ALL ABOUT ME

My Behaviour

CARYN JENNER

W
FRANKLIN WATTS
LONDON • SYDNEY

Franklin Watts
338 Euston Road
London NW1 3BH

Franklin Watts Australia
Level 17/207 Kent Street
Sydney, NSW 2000

Series editor: Sarah Peutrill
Art director: Jonathan Hair
Design: www.rawshock.co.uk
Picture researcher: Kathy Lockley
Consultant: Lisa Barton, Nurture
Group Leader

Dewey number: 302

ISBN: 978 1 4451 2977 8

Printed in China

Franklin Watts is a division of
Hachette Children's Books, an
Hachette UK company.

www.hachette.co.uk

CONTENTS

(Words in **bold** are in the glossary on page 28.)

WHAT IS BEHAVIOUR?

Behaviour is the way you act. You might change your behaviour depending on who you are with and where you are. For example, loud shouting is usually fine for the playground, but it would be bad behaviour for the classroom.

It's okay to run around and be noisy on the playground...

GOOD BEHAVIOUR

Do you like people to be nice to you? Most of us would say 'yes'! So you should behave in a nice way to other people. Being 'nice' can mean lots of different things but it always includes being kind to the people around you. It may also include being **polite**, clean and tidy.

... but in the classroom, it's usually best to stay seated and listen carefully.

When you behave well, it means that you and everyone around you gets along better and has more fun.

Do you change the way you act with different people and in different places? How?

BAD BEHAVIOUR

We call some bad behaviour 'bad **manners**', such as picking your nose in front of people, talking with your mouth full or sticking out your tongue. Being **rude** or hurtful to other people or doing anything that puts yourself or others in danger is also bad behaviour.

BEHAVIOUR AND FEELINGS

Have you noticed that behaviour and feelings are connected? Your feelings affect your actions, and your actions affect your feelings. Good behaviour makes other people feel good about you. Then you feel good about yourself.

HOW OTHERS BEHAVE

Think about how the behaviour of other people makes you feel. How do you feel if someone calls you **nasty** names? You probably won't feel very happy. But if someone helps you with your work or invites you to join their game, you'd feel happy.

Margo helps to carry Yasmin's books. Margo's helpful behaviour makes both girls feel good.

? Notice what happens when you smile at people. How do you think your smile makes them feel?

BAD MOOD BLUES

Sometimes you might feel angry or grumpy and not in a **mood** to behave well. What could you do to make yourself feel better? You could talk to someone or take some time on your own to calm down. If you make that huge effort to behave better, you might find that you feel a lot better too.

Think about who you can talk to when you're in a bad mood.

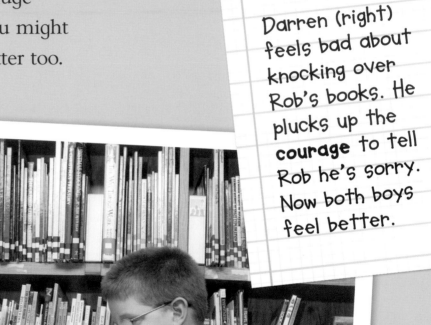

Darren (right) feels bad about knocking over Rob's books. He plucks up the **courage** to tell Rob he's sorry. Now both boys feel better.

MAGIC WORDS

Good behaviour begins with a few small words that are very special. Using these words shows that you are polite. Being polite means that you are not bossy and that you appreciate people's help or kindness.

PLEASE

Add this magic word whenever you ask for something. "Please will you help me?" "May I have a pencil please?" It's the nice way to ask for something.

THANK YOU

When someone does something nice for you, say "Thank you". If someone opens the door for you, gives you a present or lets you have a turn on the swing, remember to say "Thank you". It shows that you are grateful for their kindness.

Dawn and Stefan remember to say "please" and "thank you" to the school dinner lady. That makes the dinner lady smile.

EXCUSE ME

Say "excuse me" or "sorry" when you need to get someone's **attention**, when you bump someone or when you need to get through a crowd. When you yawn, burp or fart in front of someone you can also say "excuse me".

I'M SORRY

It's often hard to say you're sorry. It means admitting that you've done something wrong. But people think more of you if you are willing to admit your mistakes, whether you've accidentally stepped on someone's toe or you've had an **argument** with a friend.

Lucas burped after his lunch and said "excuse me" to his friends.

How does it make you feel when people say the magic words to you? How about when people don't say the magic words?

Practise saying the magic words with a role play game. Take turns to act out different examples of when to use the magic words.

A REASON FOR RULES

Why do we need rules? Imagine trying to play a game without any rules. Everyone would play the game a different way. There would be lots of confusion and probably arguments too. Rules let everyone know how to behave so that we can all work and play together in a way that keeps us happy and safe.

Nadia and her friends have fun playing together because they all know the rules of the game.

SCHOOL RULES

Many schools have a list of rules. These are often posted around the building to help you remember them. These rules are usually about safety and good behaviour. Everyone at the school must follow exactly the same rules so we all stay safe.

FOLLOWING INSTRUCTIONS

Does your teacher tell you to walk quietly in the corridors? Do your parents ask you to hurry and get ready for school? You might not like **instructions** such as these, but they help get things done safely and quickly.

School Rules

We will pay attention.

We will follow instructions.

We will raise our hands in class.

We will be kind to others.

We will keep the school tidy.

Here are some school rules. What are the rules at your school?

Why is raising hands in class a good school rule?

WITH FRIENDS

Friends are fun to be with - but even more importantly, friends are kind to each other. There's no need to do something you don't want to do or behave in a way that you don't think is right just to fit in. Good friends like you just because you're you.

MAKING NEW FRIENDS

You may have a group of best friends, but make sure to include other children as well so no one is left out. If someone seems shy or lonely, be extra-friendly. Ask that person to join you and introduce him or her to your friends. It's not only a nice thing to do, but you may also find that the new person becomes a great new friend.

Kai doesn't know Charlie very well, but he offers him a seat and they soon become friends.

Even though Kelly's team lost the match, they still congratulate the winners. Perhaps next time, they'll be the winners.

PLAYING AND SHARING

How do you feel when you don't get a turn at a game or with a particular toy? You think it's not fair, don't you? So always play fairly, and take turns and share with others. Be a good sport, too. This means don't ever cheat, and be nice to the winners even if you're disappointed that you've lost.

When you're at home, you probably just want to relax and be yourself - and that's a good thing. But you share your home with other people, so you do need to think about them as well.

Ella and her brother, Ari, take turns on the computer.

BROTHERS AND SISTERS

If you have brothers or sisters, you probably find that sometimes you're the best of friends, and other times you fight. It's hard to get along all the time. But, taking turns and sharing is just as important with family as it is with friends.

Try to sort out small disagreements before they become big problems.

GETTING ALONG

Sometimes when you're in a bad mood, you might behave badly towards your family. But that's not fair. If you feel like this try to talk about your feelings before you start shouting at anyone!

RULES AT HOME

You'll have rules at home to follow too. Sometimes you might have to help with the chores. You can help your parents or carers by being tidy and doing the chores they ask you to. It may be boring but if everyone helps out, it all gets done quicker.

It's Eve's job to help her dad tidy up the kitchen. They make a good team.

What changes can you make to your behaviour to help you get along better with your family?

When you're out and about you want to stay safe, so you've got to think extra-hard about your behaviour and keep out of danger. You also need to take extra care of the places you go.

STAY SAFE

Make sure your parents or carers always know where you are. If you run off without telling anyone, you could get lost. Never go anywhere with people you don't know.

When a stranger offers them a lift, Matthew and Sophie walk home quickly and tell their mum.

ROAD SAFETY

Roads can be dangerous places so be careful and walk on safe paths or pavements. Only cross the road at safe places, such as zebra crossings or pelican crossings, and remember to look both ways for traffic. Wear bright clothes or reflectors so you can be seen in the dark, and always wear a safety helmet when you ride your bike.

Agata and Bartek always look both ways before they cross the road.

Sean saved his banana skin until he could find a bin in the park.

DON'T LITTER!

Don't be a litter bug - hold on to your rubbish until you find a bin to put it in.

How do you feel when you see rubbish everywhere?

BE PATIENT

Being patient can be hard. But if everyone wanted everything *right this minute* there would be a lot of bad tempers. Being patient shows that you are thinking of other people.

Ricardo doesn't like being at the back of the **queue**, but he knows he must wait his turn.

WAITING

It may seem that you're always waiting for something - waiting in queues; waiting for your teacher to call on you; waiting for your mum or dad to take you out; waiting for your turn on the swing. Waiting is not easy, but be patient and your turn will come. No one likes queuing but it does mean everyone gets a fair turn.

Jody interrupts her mum on the telephone, but her mum asks her to wait till she's finished.

DON'T INTERRUPT

When someone is speaking, be patient and wait until the person is finished before you speak. This is also important if someone is speaking on the telephone. Only **interrupt** if there is an emergency.

What can you do to help time pass more quickly when you are waiting? For example, you could make up a story, count backwards or play a quiet game such as 'I Spy'.

DON'T BE RUDE

When you behave rudely, you show that you don't care how the people around you feel. Isn't it better to be polite so that people enjoy being with you?

DISGUSTING BEHAVIOUR

Try not to burp or fart in front of other people, and certainly don't pick your nose. There's no point trying to use disgusting behaviour to show off. It doesn't work. You might think this sort of behaviour is funny, but it isn't at all nice for the people around you.

DON'T SPREAD GERMS

Germs make people ill. Catch germs by covering your mouth when you cough and your nose when you sneeze. Use a tissue to catch sneezes, blow your nose or wipe a drippy nose. When you are finished with the tissue, put it in a bin and wash your hands as soon as you can.

Ah-tishoo! Ryan quickly catches his sneeze in a tissue.

TABLE MANNERS

Table manners aren't hard to learn. You get to practise them three times a day!

Why do you think table manners are important?

Here's a reminder of how to eat politely:

- Stay in your seat. If you must get up, say "excuse me".
- Use your fork, knife and spoon to eat, not your hands (unless it's a sandwich or other 'finger foods'!).
- Wipe sticky fingers and mucky mouth on a paper napkin or tissue, not on your clothes.
- Eat with your mouth closed.
- Remember to use your magic words when you ask for or are given something.

Jamal uses table manners at school, at home and anywhere he eats.

NASTY BEHAVIOUR

Nasty behaviour hurts people. Hitting, kicking, punching or pinching is NOT okay. Nor is lying, stealing or cheating. You don't like people to hurt you, do you? So don't do it to others.

? Brendan tries to ignore Fred's teasing. How do you think Brendan feels? What can he do about Fred's **bullying**?

BULLYING

A bully is someone who tries to feel powerful by picking on someone else over and over again. Sometimes a bully might hit and kick to hurt someone, or tease and make fun to hurt their feelings. If you tease someone, you might think it's just a harmless joke. But it's not harmless if you hurt someone's feelings. You don't like someone bullying you, so don't do it to others. If you are being bullied, tell an adult that you trust.

Oliver thinks it's funny to pull his sister's hair — but she doesn't like it!

RIGHT OR WRONG?

Some people think that nasty behaviour is okay, as long as they don't get caught. For example, if you steal sweets from the shop or cheat on a spelling test and don't get caught, does that mean it's okay? The answer is a firm NO, it's not okay! You've still done something wrong and that kind of behaviour is not honest or fair.

Amira tells her teacher when she sees two other children fighting. Miss Kowalski will stop the fight and help the children sort out their differences.

? Why should you tell a parent, teacher or other adult if you see nasty behaviour?

YOU'RE IN CONTROL...

Only *you* control how *you* behave. Think about the choices you make about your behaviour. How will your behaviour affect yourself and other people? How will it make you feel about yourself?

? Hal wants the other children to climb on the tables too. What would you do? Why?

MAKING CHOICES

Sometimes, people react too quickly without thinking about what they are doing. For example, if someone gave you a shove, your first reaction might be to shove back. But that's not a good choice, is it? Instead, you could choose to keep calm and either tell an adult what happened or ignore it.

These children show good behaviour on their school trip. They've made the right choice, and everyone has a good time.

If you get your behaviour wrong, say you're sorry and mean it. Then try to make a better choice next time.

THINK BEFORE YOU ACT

No one can behave their best every minute of the day, not even adults. But if you think before you act, and treat other people the way you like to be treated, you're more likely to make the right choices about your behaviour. You'll be happier, and so will everyone around you.

GLOSSARY

Appreciate be grateful for.

Argument having an argument means not agreeing or getting along, fighting.

Attention taking notice of somebody or something. Paying attention means listening carefully.

Behaviour how you act.

Bullying hurting or making fun of other people in order to feel powerful.

Courage bravery.

Instructions directions on what to do and how to do it.

Interrupt wanting attention when someone is already speaking or doing something else.

Manners behaving in a polite way, being kind and helpful.

Mood how a person is feeling.

Nasty hurtful.

Patient willing to wait. It is polite to be patient.

Polite showing respect for other people, for example using words such as 'please' and 'thank you'.

Queue a line where people wait their turn.

Rude unkind, not showing respect for other people.

FURTHER INFORMATION

Websites

Kidscape - preventing bullying, protecting children
www.kidscape.org.uk

Childline - counselling service for children and young people
www.childline.org.uk

Family Links - transforming schools and families
www.familylinks.org.uk

The Place 2 Be - school-based counselling service, dedicated to improving the emotional wellbeing of children, their families and the whole school community.
www.theplace2be.org.uk

Note to parents and teachers: Every effort has been made by the Publishers to ensure that these websites are suitable for children, that they are of the highest educational value, and that they contain no inappropriate or offensive material. However, because of the nature of the Internet, it is impossible to guarantee that the contents of these sites will not be altered. We strongly advise that Internet access is supervised by a responsible adult.

Books

'Why Manners Matter' series: *At Home, At School, Playing in the Park, Going Shopping* (Franklin Watts)

'*How Should I Behave?* by Mick Manning and Brita Granstrom (Franklin Watts)

Excuse Me, I Don't Care, I'll Do It It Wasn't Me by Brian Moses and Mike Gordon (Wayland)

Why Should I Share?, Why Should I Help?, Why Should I Listen? by Clare Llewellyn and Mike Gordon (Wayland)

'Taking Part' series: *A Caring School* by Sally Hewitt (Franklin Watts)

'Good and Bad' series: *Thief, Selfish, Moody, Liar, Cheat, Bully* by Janine Amos (Evans)

INDEX